Orton Gillingham Red Words

Orton Gillingham activities and resources to help children read and write

VOLUME 2

Adriana Robertson

INTRODUCTION

Dyslexia is a neurodevelopmental disorder that manifests itself in those who have difficulties learning to read through conventional means and techniques. Dyslexia can be described as a learning disability that appears during the early stages of development and presents differently as the person grows older. These problems tend to appear during childhood and can persist throughout the person's adolescence and even adulthood.

Why Phonological Awareness Is Effective

In the same way that, in order to learn how to do number operations we must first understand that a number is the graphic representation of a value, when learning to read, certain skill sets need to be acquired before starting to read. Not all children develop these skills equally; many times they begin learning to read without being prepared for it.

Training phonological awareness allows the student to understand the segmental structure of language and develop their abilities to discriminate, categorize, associate and synthesize linguistic information.

How to develop a phonological awareness program

Phonological awareness must be instructed in order to be effective, so the first thing when treating a child with dyslexia is to conduct a good evaluation. Once evaluated in level, we will know what the child's greatest difficulties are when it comes to writing and reading.

Red Word Practice – and

Dip and Dab.

and

Read and write.

Write the missing letters.

Find and circle – **and**.

and	go
it	a
and	and

Write a sentence using the sight word- **and**.

Red Word Practice - look

Dip and Dab.

look

Read and write.

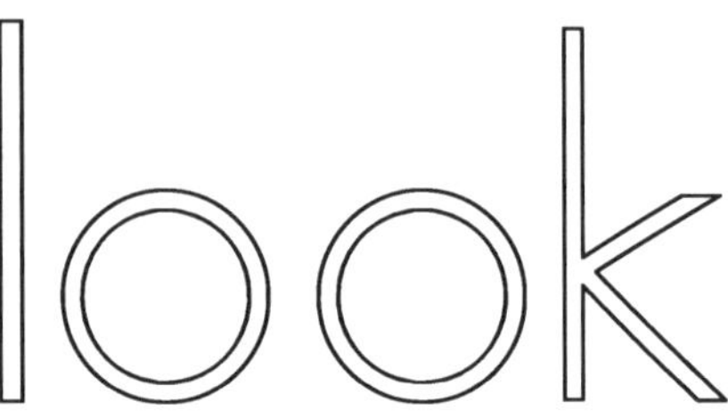

look look

Write the missing letters.

__ __ __ __

Find and circle - look.

can	look
look	you
look	to

Write a sentence using the sight word- look.

Red Word Practice — is

Dip and Dab.

is

Read and write.

is

is is

Write the missing letters.

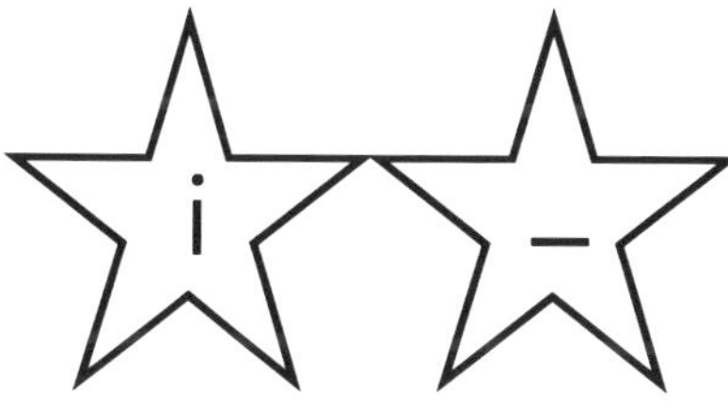

_ _

Find and circle – **is**.

is	is
to	can
a	is

Write a sentence using the sight word- **is**.

Red Word Practice - the

Dip and Dab.

the

Read and write.

the the

Write the missing letters.

Find and circle - **the**.

to	the
here	the
the	me

Write a sentence using the sight word- **the**.

Red Word Practice - run

Dip and Dab.

run

Read and write.

run run

Write the missing letters.

___ ___ ___

Find and circle - **run.**

run	can
run	you
red	run

Write a sentence using the sight word- **run.**

Red Word Practice — find

Dip and Dab.

find

Read and write.

find find

Write the missing letters.

f i _ d

___ ___ ___ ___

Find and circle – **find**.

me	play
here	find
find	find

Write a sentence using the sight word- **find**.

Red Word Practice - my

Dip and Dab.

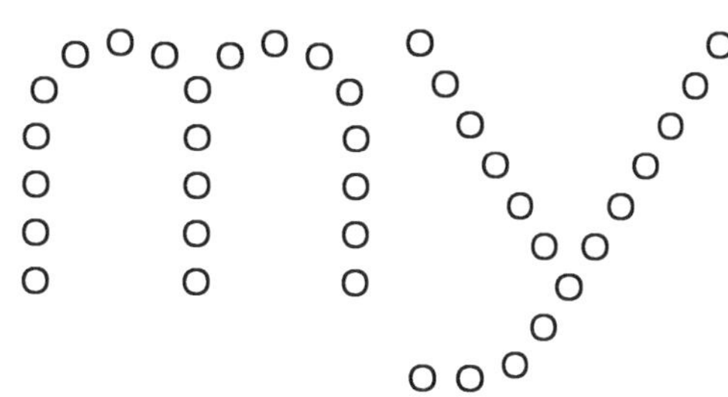

Read and write.

my my

Write the missing letters.

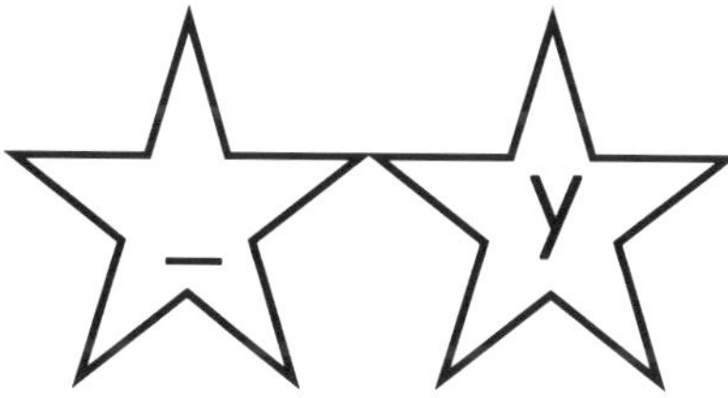

Find and circle - **my**.

my	one
my	go
big	my

Write a sentence using the sight word- **my**.

Red Word Practice up

Dip and Dab.

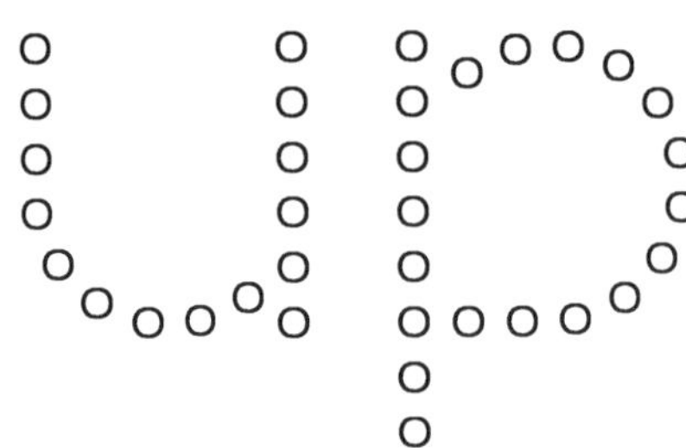

Read and write.

up up

Write the missing letters.

_ _

Find and circle - **up**.

up	my
help	up
up	are

Write a sentence using the sight word- **up**.

Red Word Practice - come

Dip and Dab.

come

Read and write.

come

come come

Write the missing letters.

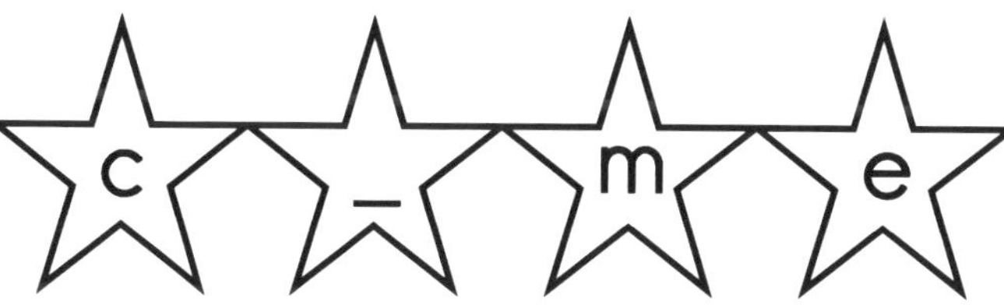

__ __ __ __

Find and circle - **come.**

come	find
go	come
not	come

Write a sentence using the sight word- **come.**

Red Word Practice – big

Dip and Dab.

big

Read and write.

big big

Write the missing letters.

___ ___ ___

Find and circle – big.

big	for
big	big
jump	it

Write a sentence using the sight word- big.

Red Word Practice — can

Dip and Dab.

can

Read and write.

can can

Write the missing letters.

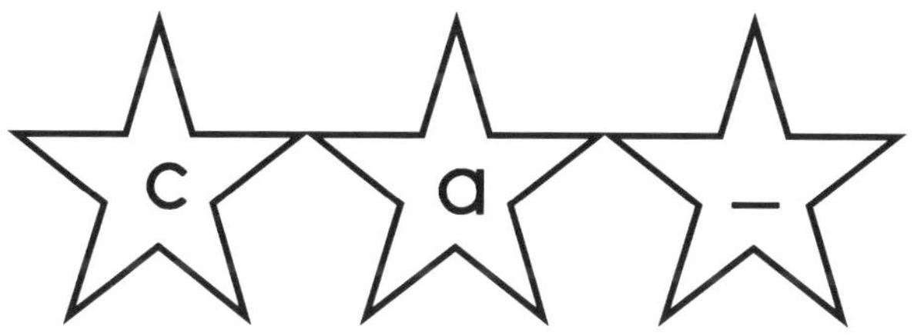

__ __ __

Find and circle – **can**.

can	it
can	for
are	can

Write a sentence using the sight word- **can**.

Red Word Practice - go

Dip and Dab.

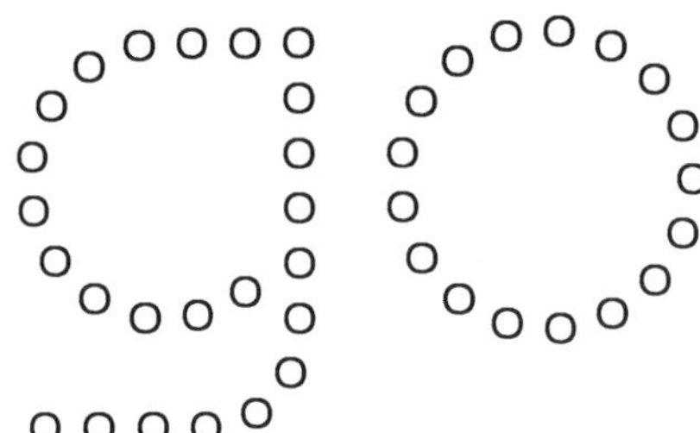

Read and write.

go go

Write the missing letters.

_ _

Find and circle - **go**.

go	go
are	we
I	go

Write a sentence using the sight word- **go**.

Red Word Practice — me

Dip and Dab.

me

Read and write.

me

me me

Write the missing letters.

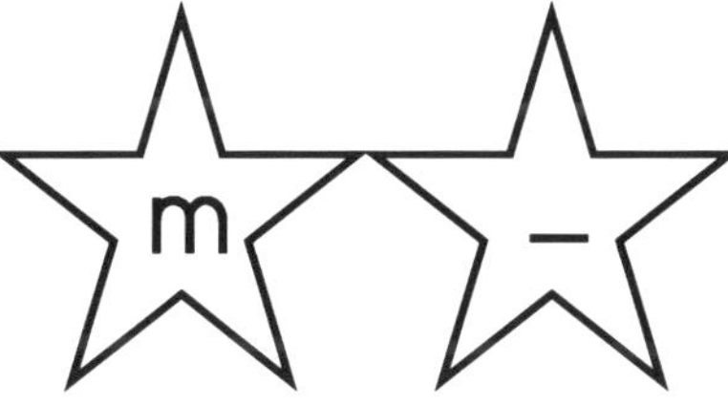

_ _

Find and circle – **me**.

look	red
me	me
blue	can

Write a sentence using the sight word- **me**.

Red Word Practice — it

Dip and Dab.

Read and write.

it it

Write the missing letters.

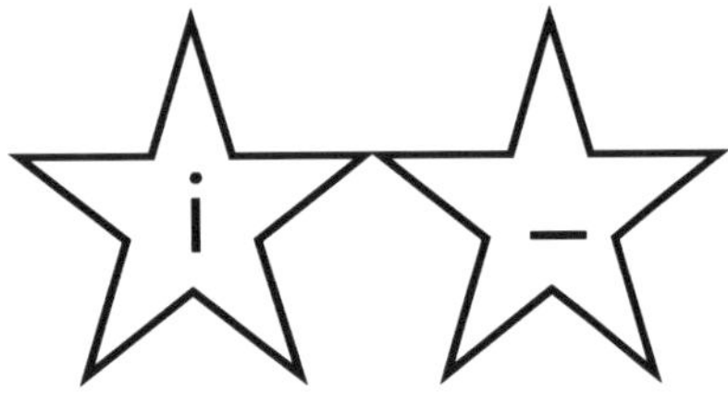

__ __

Find and circle – **it**.

it	help
go	it
it	it

Write a sentence using the sight word- **it**.

Red Word Practice - see

Dip and Dab.

see

Read and write.

see

see see

Write the missing letters.

_ _ _

Find and circle - **see**.

the	see
see	down
red	see

Write a sentence using the sight word- **see**.

Red Word Practice - for

Dip and Dab.

for

Read and write.

for for

Write the missing letters.

__ __ __

Find and circle - for.

for	for
can	for
go	said

Write a sentence using the sight word- for.

Red Word Practice - three

Dip and Dab.

three

Read and write.

three three

Write the missing letters.

Find and circle - three.

three	to
find	three
here	three

Write a sentence using the sight word- three.

Red Word Practice - away

Dip and Dab.

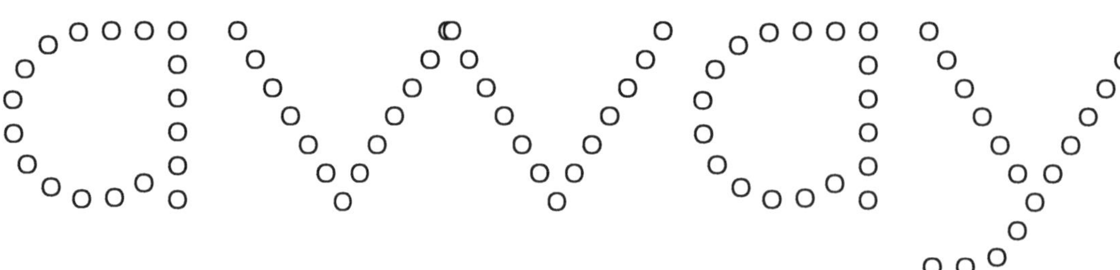

Read and write.

away away

Write the missing letters.

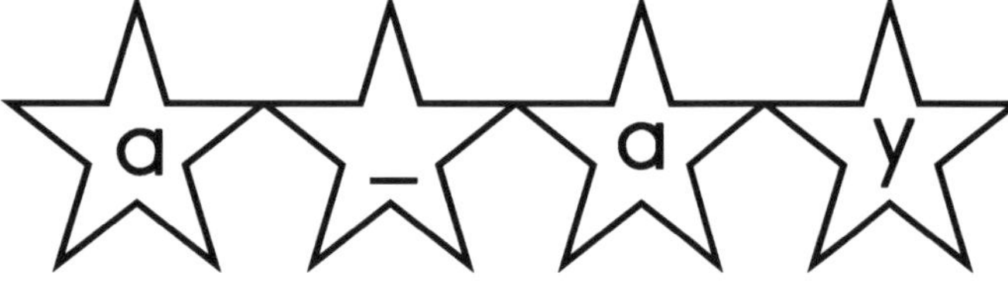

Find and circle - **away**.

are	go
away	away
away	red

Write a sentence using the sight word- **away**.

Red Word Practice - here

Dip and Dab.

here

Read and write.

here here

Write the missing letters.

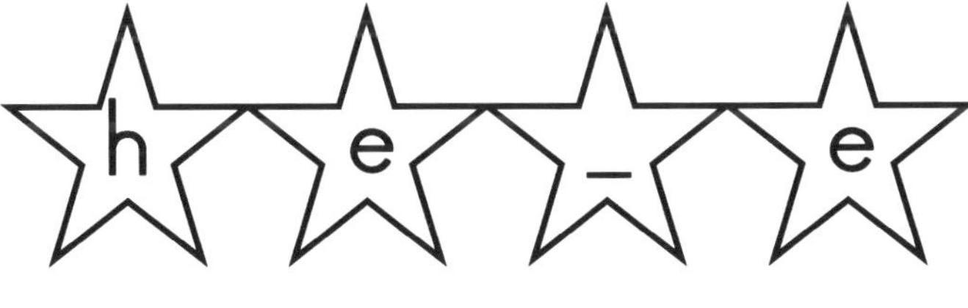

_ _ _ _

Find and circle - **here**.

help	go
here	here
red	here

Write a sentence using the sight word- **here**.

Red Word Practice - one

Dip and Dab.

one

Read and write.

one one

Write the missing letters.

__ __ __

Find and circle - **one**.

one	where
jump	one
red	one

Write a sentence using the sight word- **one**.

Red Word Practice - to

Dip and Dab.

to

Read and write.

to to

Write the missing letters.

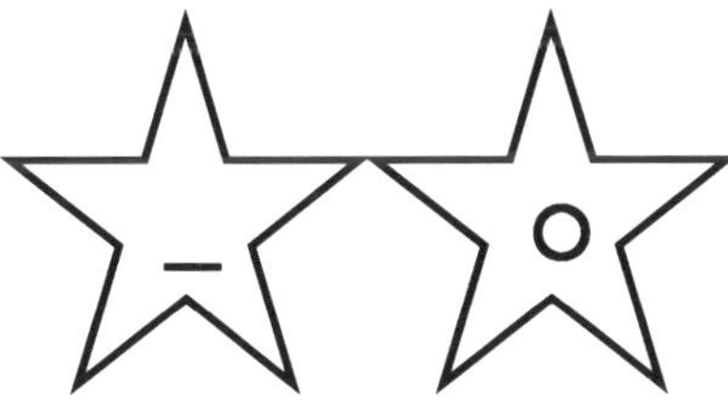

_ _

Find and circle - **to**.

make	to
said	you
to	to

Write a sentence using the sight word- **to**.

Red Word Practice - blue

Dip and Dab.

blue

Read and write.

blue blue

Write the missing letters.

_ _ _ _

Find and circle - **blue**.

blue	we
blue	can
blue	jump

Write a sentence using the sight word- **blue**.

Red Word Practice – jump

Dip and Dab.

jump

Read and write.

jump jump

Write the missing letters.

_ _ _ _

Find and circle – jump.

find	funny
jump	to
red	jump

Write a sentence using the sight word– jump.

Red Word Practice - two

Dip and Dab.

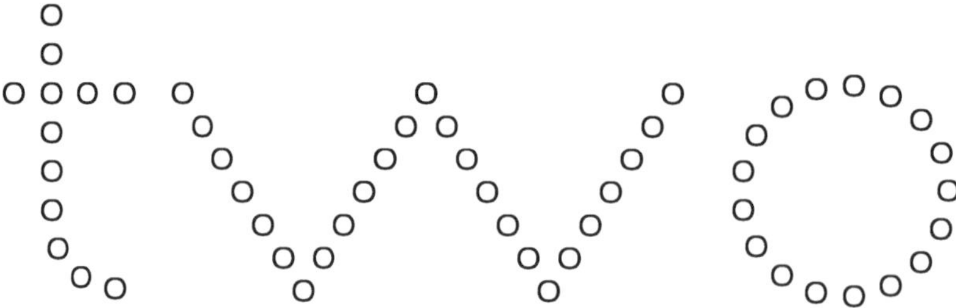

Read and write.

two **two**

Write the missing letters.

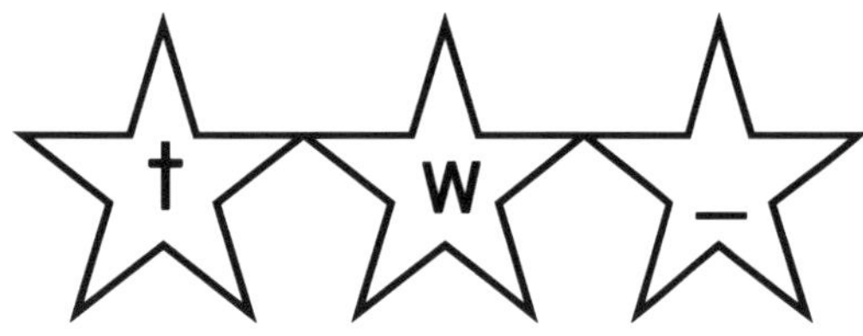

___ ___ ___

Find and circle - **two.**

two	are
one	two
two	little

Write a sentence using the sight word- **two.**

Red Word Practice - in

Dip and Dab.

in

Read and write.

in

in	in

Write the missing letters.

__ __

Find and circle – **in**.

in	I
are	in
to	in

Write a sentence using the sight word- **in**.

Red Word Practice — we

Dip and Dab.

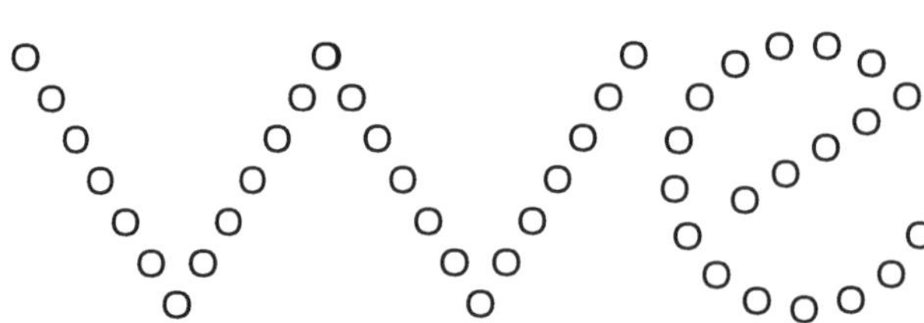

Read and write.

we **we**

Write the missing letters.

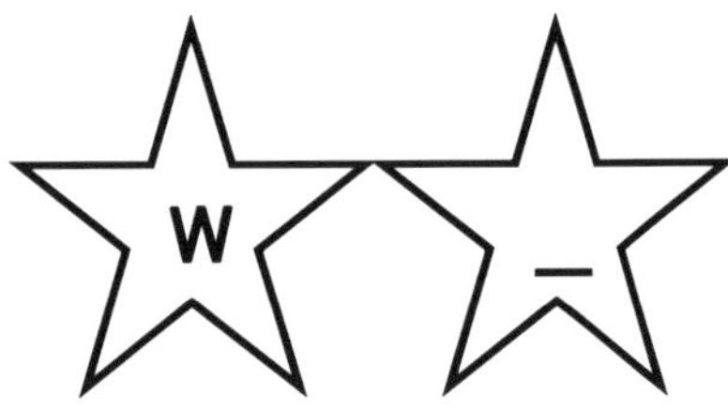

Find and circle – **we**.

we	little
a	we
we	three

Write a sentence using the sight word- **we**.

Red Word Practice - funny

Dip and Dab.

funny

Read and write.

funny funny

Write the missing letters.

Find and circle - funny.

big	funny
funny	jump
run	funny

Write a sentence using the sight word- funny.

Red Word Practice — where

Dip and Dab.

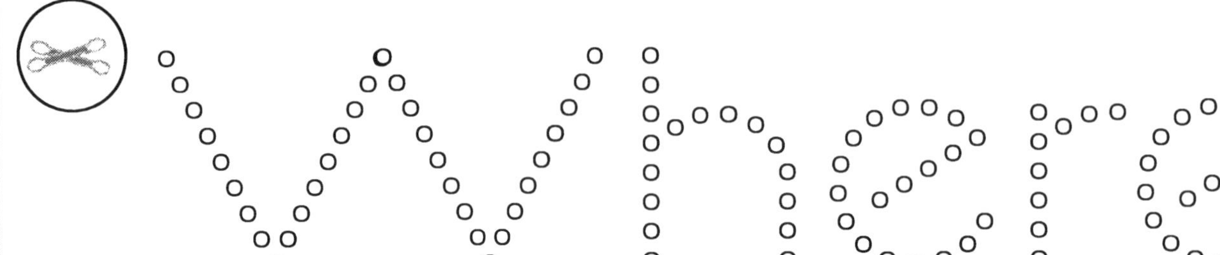

Read and write.

where where

Write the missing letters.

__ __ __ __ __

Find and circle – **where.**

we	where
where	not
where	red

Write a sentence using the sight word- **where.**

Red Word Practice — I

Dip and Dab.

Read and write.

I I

Write the missing letters.

_

Find and circle – I.

I	I
we	go
help	I

Write a sentence using the sight word- I.

Red Word Practice — you

Dip and Dab.

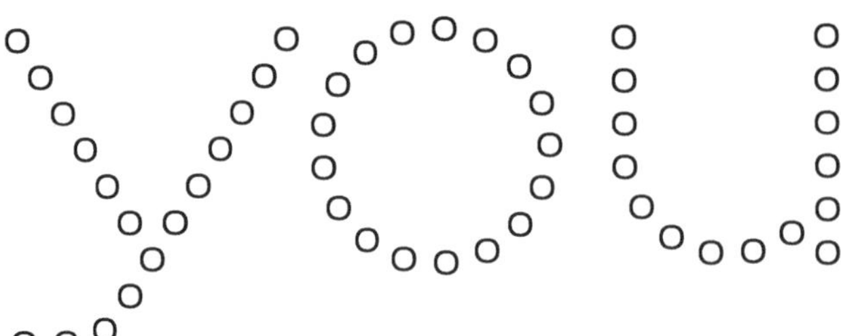

Read and write.

you you

Write the missing letters.

Find and circle – **you**.

you	can
little	you
you	red

Write a sentence using the sight word– **you**.

Red Word Practice - not

Dip and Dab.

not

Read and write.

not not

Write the missing letters.

__ __ __

Find and circle - you.

for	not
not	can
not	little

Write a sentence using the sight word- not.

Red Word Practice — said

Dip and Dab.

said

Read and write.

said	said

Write the missing letters.

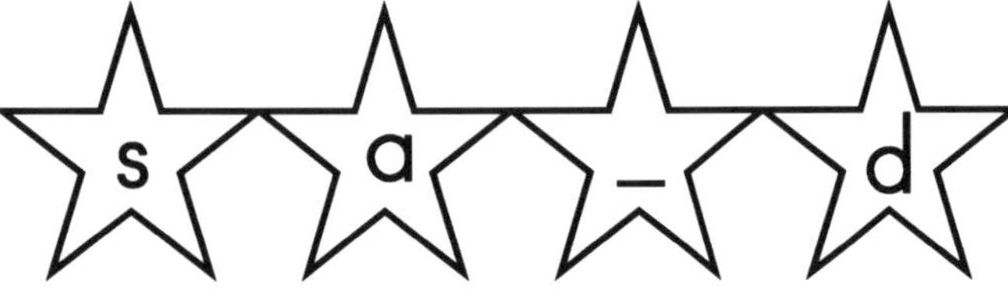

__ __ __ __

Find and circle – **said.**

said	jump
said	said
here	funny

Write a sentence using the sight word- **said.**

Red Word Practice - a

Dip and Dab.

Read and write.

a a

Write the missing letters.

_

Find and circle - a.

a	play
a	run
look	a

Write a sentence using the sight word- a.

Red Word Practice - red

Dip and Dab.

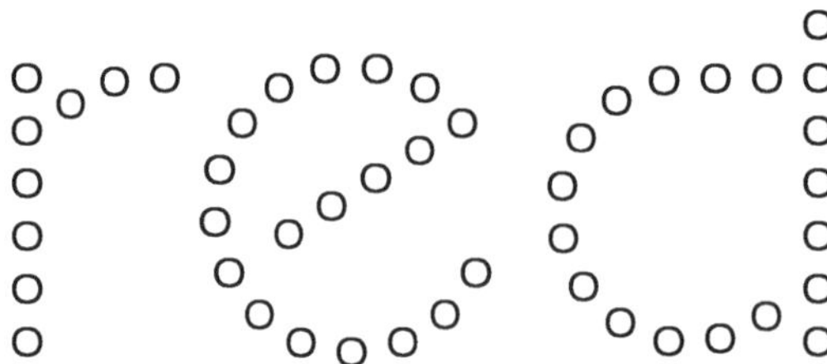

Read and write.

red red

Write the missing letters.

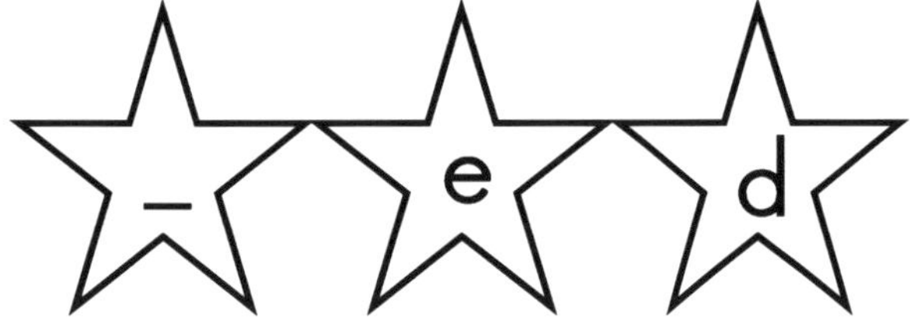

__ __ __

Find and circle - **red**.

it	red
find	red
red	me

Write a sentence using the sight word- **red**.

Red Word Practice - make

Dip and Dab.

make

Read and write.

make make

Write the missing letters.

_ _ _ _

Find and circle - **make**.

make	run
up	make
it	make

Write a sentence using the sight word- **make**.

Red Word Practice - little

Dip and Dab.

little

Read and write.

little little

Write the missing letters.

Find and circle - little.

little	little
jump	little
we	can

Write a sentence using the sight word- little.

Red Word Practice help

Dip and Dab.

help

Read and write.

help help

Write the missing letters.

__ __ __ __

Find and circle – help.

down	is
help	help
look	help

Write a sentence using the sight word- help.

Red Word Practice – down

Dip and Dab.

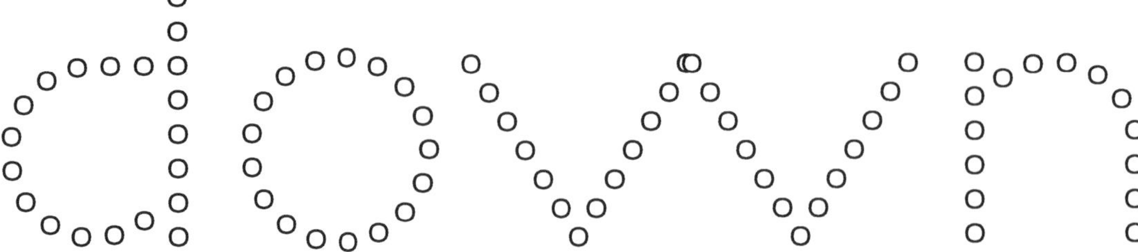

Read and write.

down down

Write the missing letters.

d _ w n

_ _ _ _

Find and circle – **down**.

down	down
is	little
down	play

Write a sentence using the sight word- **down**.

Red Word Practice - play

Dip and Dab.

play

Read and write.

play play

Write the missing letters.

_ _ _ _

Find and circle - play.

play	look
find	play
come	play

Write a sentence using the sight word- play.

Red Word Practice - yellow

Dip and Dab.

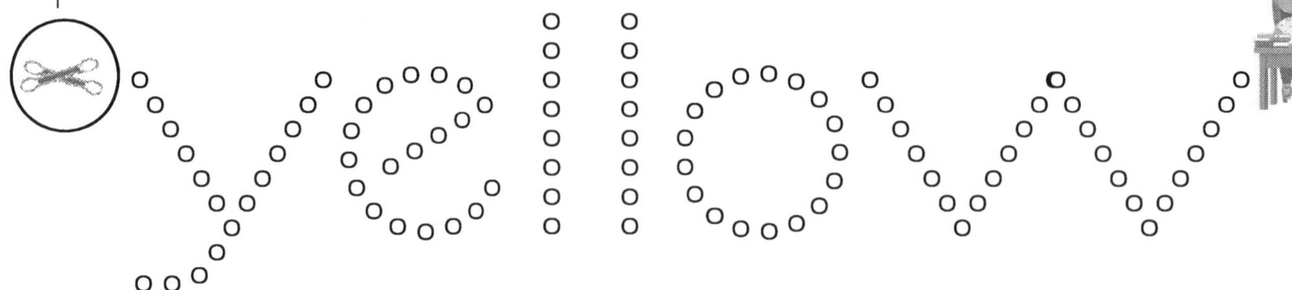

Read and write.

yellow yellow

Write the missing letters.

Find and circle - yellow.

is	yellow
yellow	play
red	yellow

Write a sentence using the sight word- yellow.

Red Word Practice — and

Red Word Practice — look

Read the sentence and color the picture.

Look at the rainbow.

Cut and paste to spell the sight word.

look

k o l o

Red Word Practice — is

Read the sentence and color the picture.

This is my school bag.

Cut and paste to spell the sight word.

is

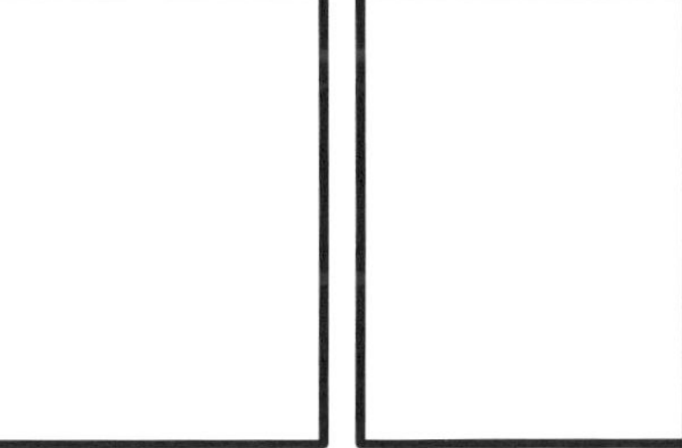

s i

Red Word Practice - the

Read the sentence and color the picture.

There is lion at the zoo.

Cut and paste to spell the sight word.

the

h t e

Red Word Practice - run

Read the sentence and color the picture.

Cut and paste to spell the sight word.

run

n r u

Red Word Practice find

Read the sentence and color the picture.

I can't find the jam.

Cut and paste to spell the sight word.

find

d i f n

Red Word Practice — my

Read the sentence and color the picture.

My socks are red.

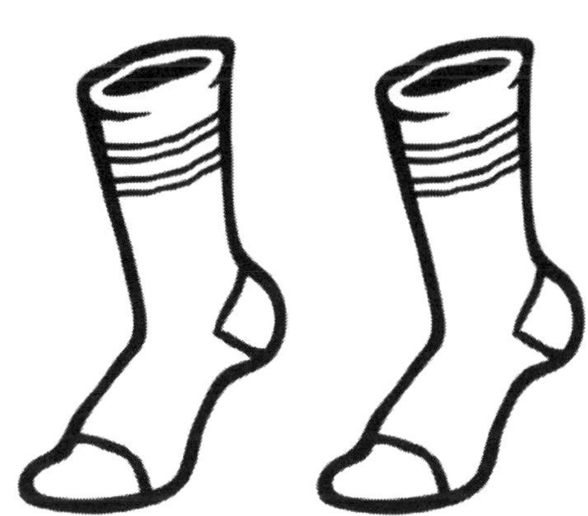

Cut and paste to spell the sight word.

my 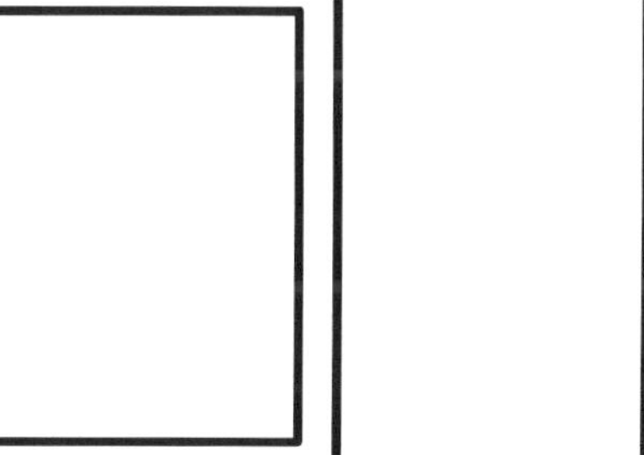

y m

Red Word Practice — up

Read the sentence and color the picture.

Birds fly up in the sky.

Cut and paste to spell the sight word.

up

p u

Red Word Practice — come

Read the sentence and color the picture.

Will you come to the park?

Cut and paste to spell the sight word.

come

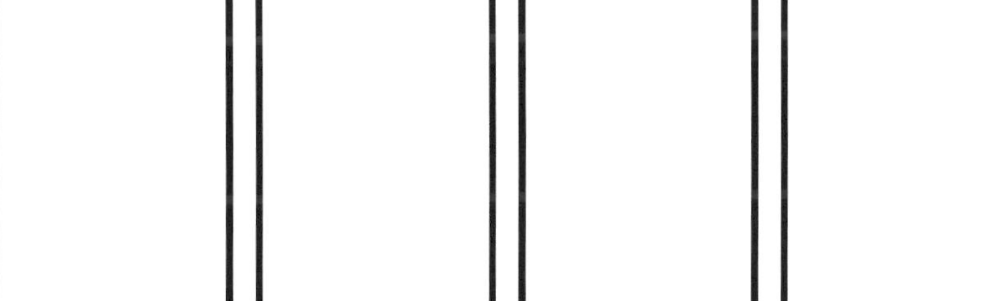

o m e c

Red Word Practice – big

Read the sentence and color the picture.

This is a big bus.

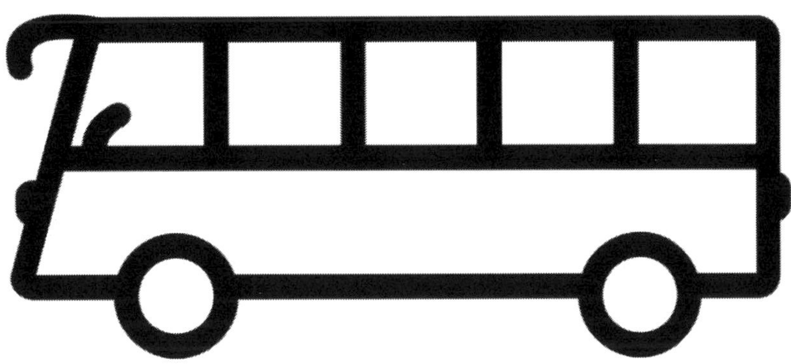

Cut and paste to spell the sight word.

big

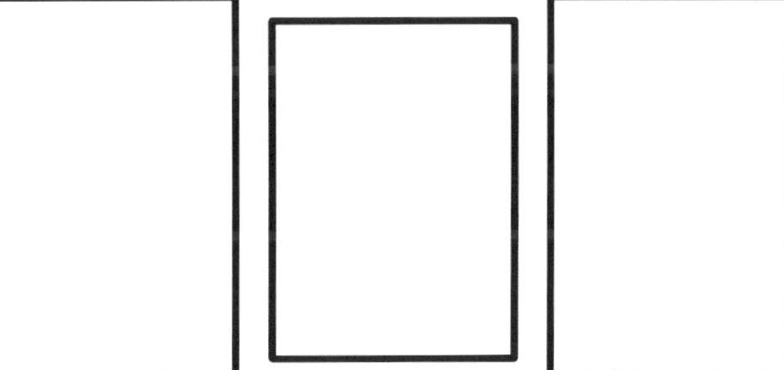

i g b

Red Word Practice — can

Read the sentence and color the picture.

Can I borrow your pen ?

Cut and paste to spell the sight word.

can

n a c

Red Word Practice — go

Read the sentence and color the picture.

I go to school.

Cut and paste to spell the sight word.

go

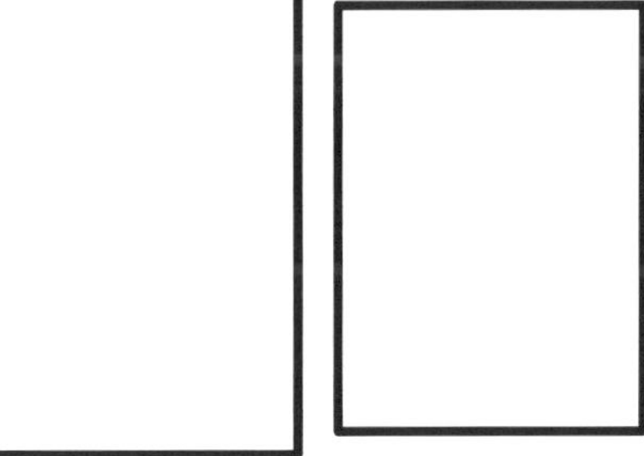

Red Word Practice — me

Read the sentence and color the picture.

Will you play with me?

Cut and paste to spell the sight word.

me 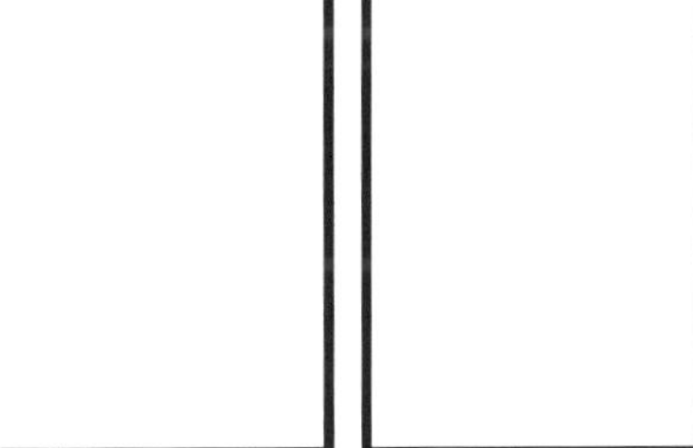

e m

Red Word Practice - it

Read the sentence and color the picture.

It is my guitar.

Cut and paste to spell the sight word.

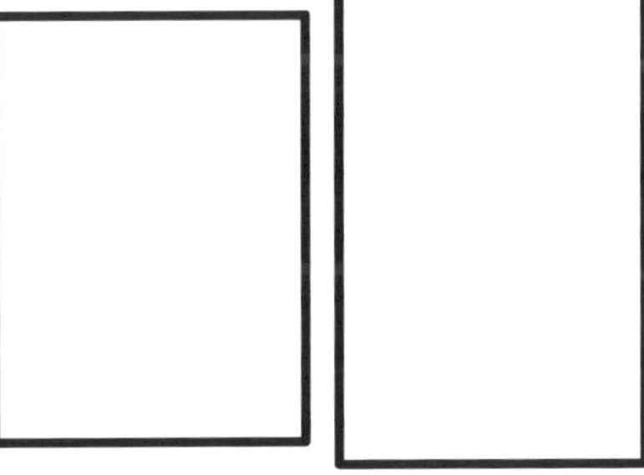

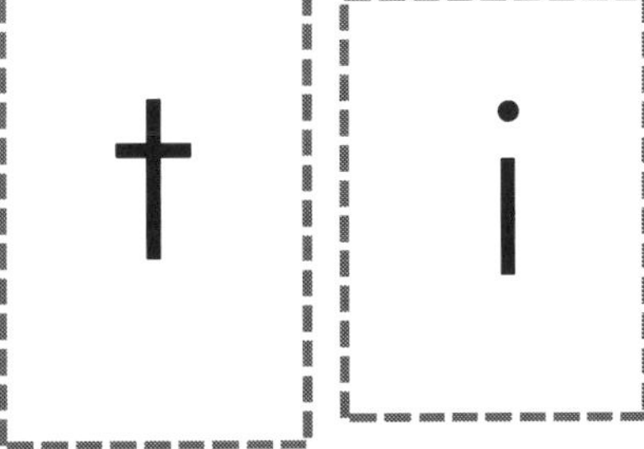

Red Word Practice — see

Read the sentence and color the picture.

I see a fish.

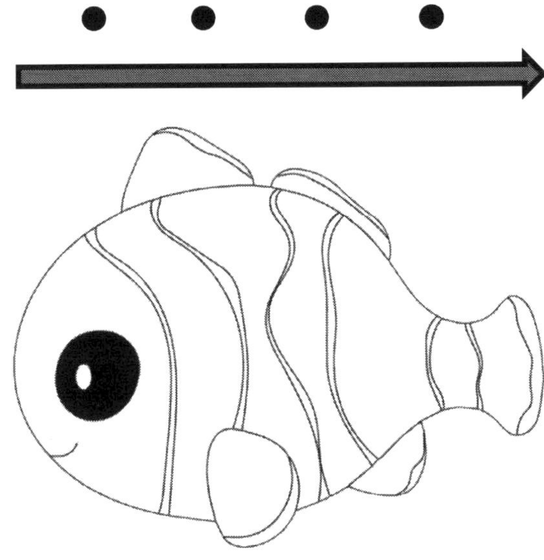

Cut and paste to spell the sight word.

see

e s e

Red Word Practice for

Read the sentence and color the picture.

Apples are good for your health.

Cut and paste to spell the sight word.

for

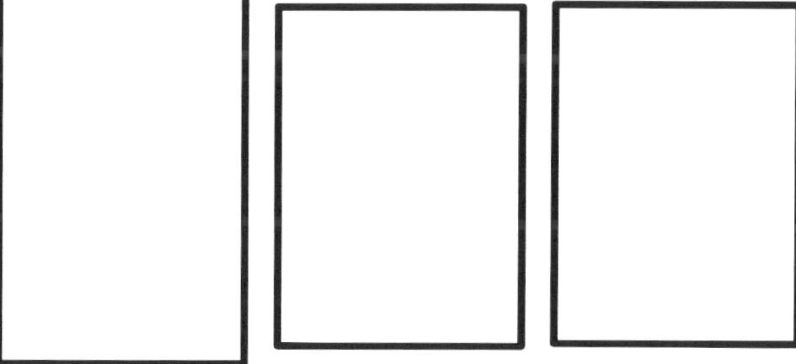

o r f

Red Word Practice — three

Read the sentence and color the picture.

I have three books.

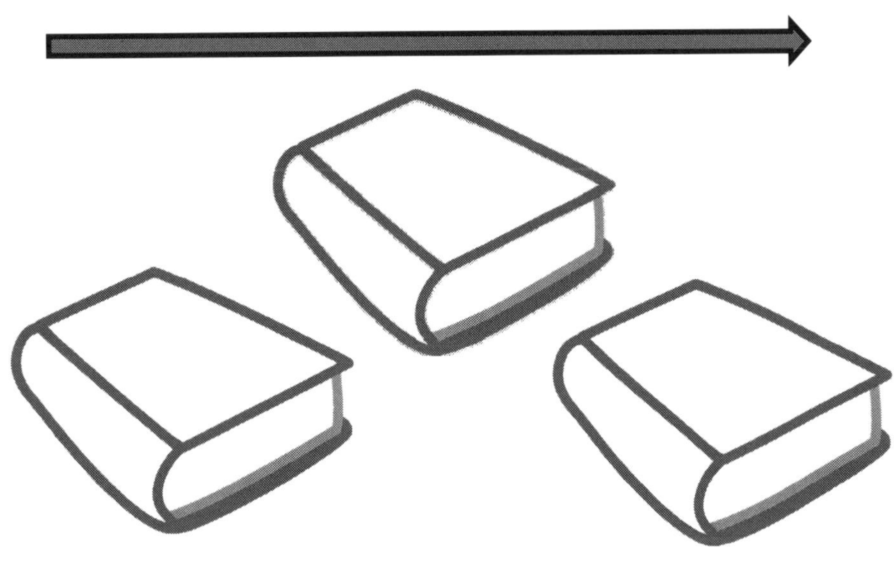

Cut and paste to spell the sight word.

three

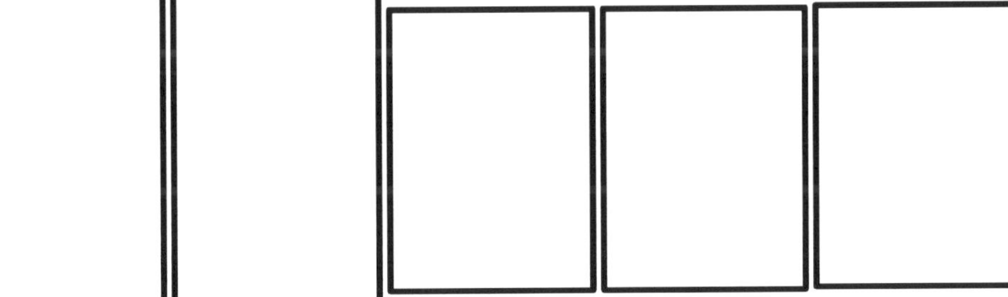

e r h e t

Red Word Practice — away

Read the sentence and color the picture.

Her dog ran away.

Cut and paste to spell the sight word.

away

y w a a

Red Word Practice – here

Read the sentence and color the picture.

Here is a fan.

Cut and paste to spell the sight word.

here

h r e e

Red Word Practice — one

Read the sentence and color the picture.

I have one kite.

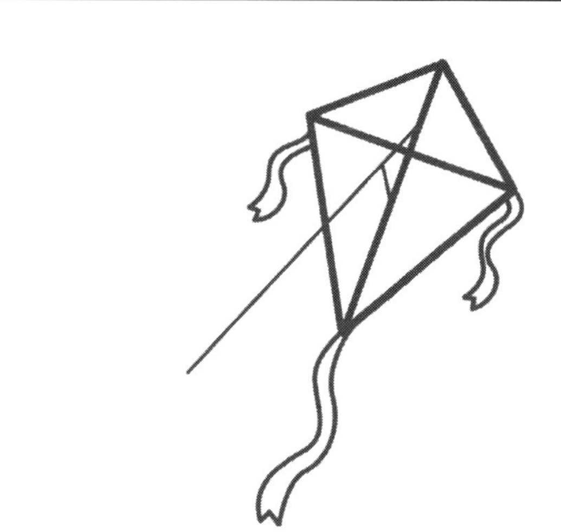

Cut and paste to spell the sight word.

e o n

Red Word Practice — to

Read the sentence and color the picture.

I went to the shop.

Cut and paste to spell the sight word.

to

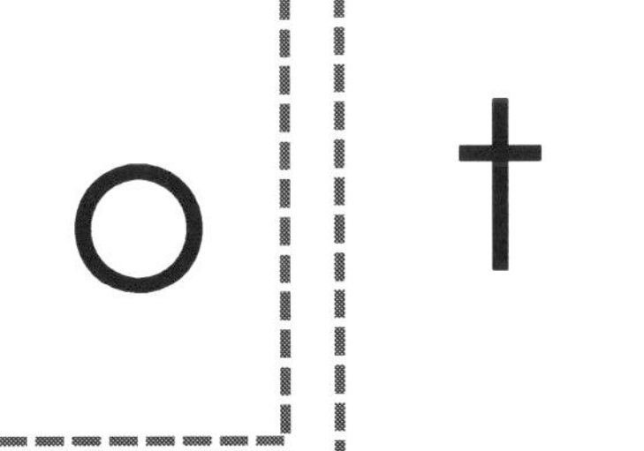

Red Word Practice blue

Read the sentence and color the picture.

I have a blue mat.

Cut and paste to spell the sight word.

blue

e l u b

Red Word Practice - jump

Read the sentence and color the picture.

The green frog can jump.

Cut and paste to spell the sight word.

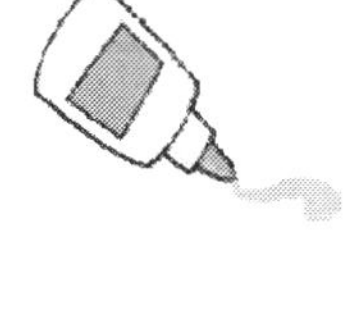

jump

m j u p

Red Word Practice — two

Read the sentence and color the picture.

There are two giraffes at the zoo.

Cut and paste to spell the sight word.

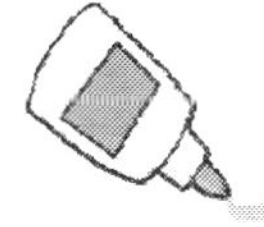

two

Red Word Practice in

Read the sentence and color the picture.

Cut and paste to spell the sight word.

in

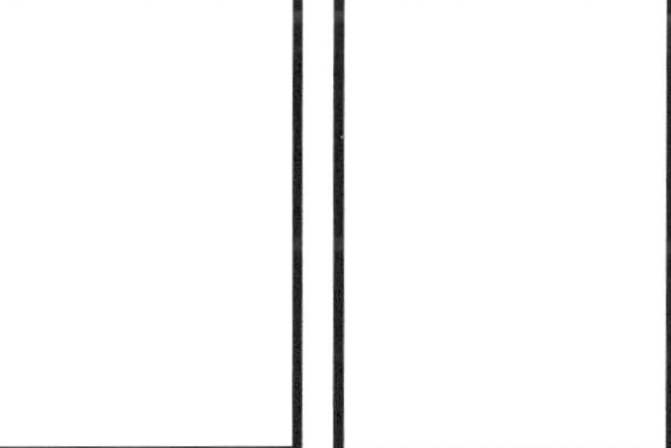

n i

Red Word Practice — we

Read the sentence and color the picture.

We are going to school by bus.

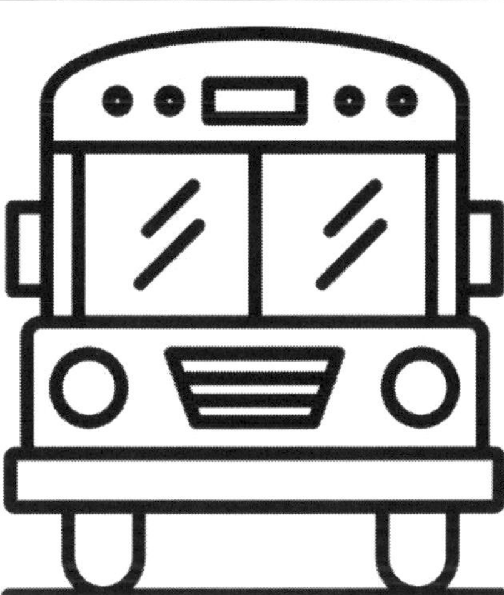

Cut and paste to spell the sight word.

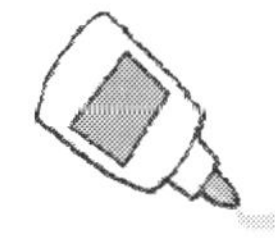

we

e w

Red Word Practice — funny

Read the sentence and color the picture.

Sam is a very funny person.

Cut and paste to spell the sight word.

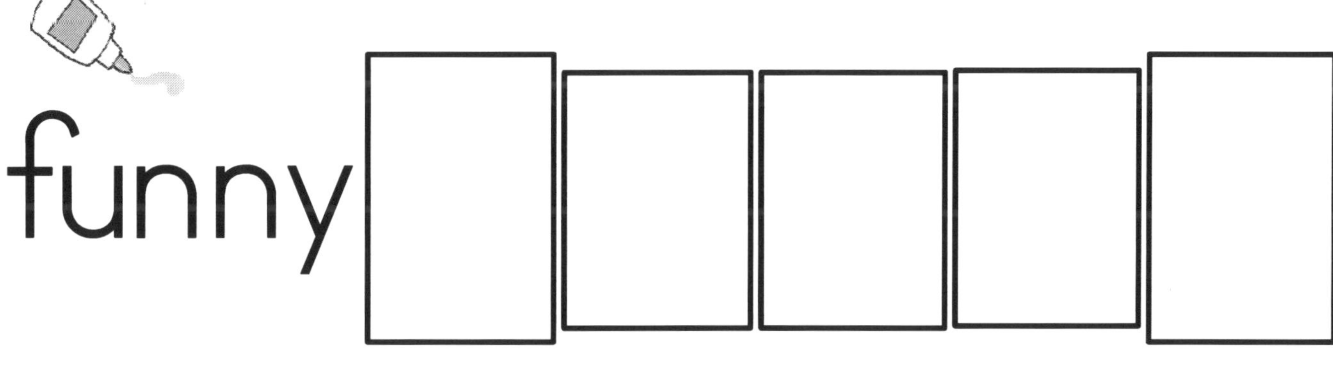

n u y n f

Red Word Practice — where

Read the sentence and color the picture.

Where is my cat.

Cut and paste to spell the sight word.

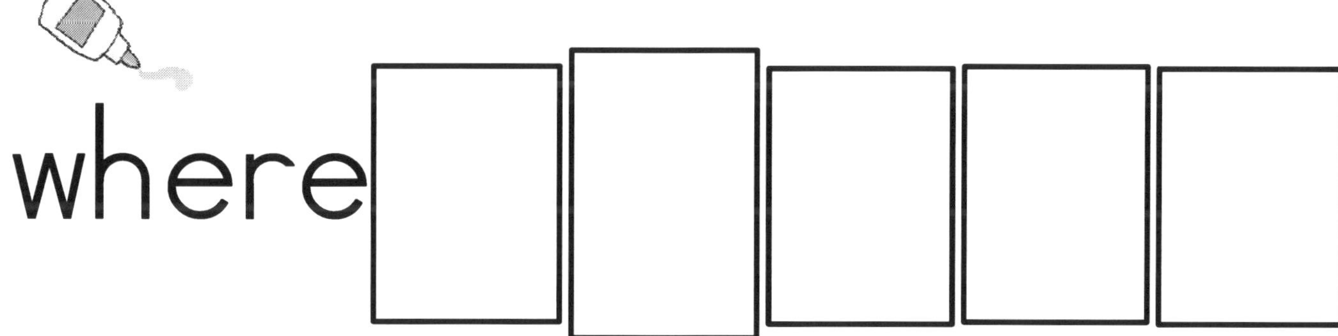

r e h w e

Red Word Practice — I

Read the sentence and color the picture.

I like to eat ice-cream.

Cut and paste to spell the sight word.

I 

Red Word Practice — you

Read the sentence and color the picture.

You are a good player.

Cut and paste to spell the sight word.

you

o y u

Red Word Practice — not

Read the sentence and color the picture.

We can not go home.

Cut and paste to spell the sight word.

not

o t n

Red Word Practice — said

Read the sentence and color the picture.

Mom said, "Sit on the rug".

Cut and paste to spell the sight word.

said

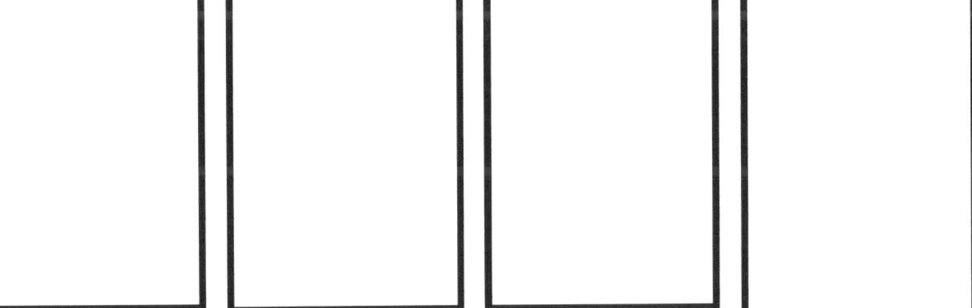

d i a s

Red Word Practice - a

Read the sentence and color the picture.

I need a cup of coffee.

Cut and paste to spell the sight word.

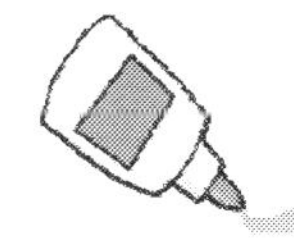

a 

a

Red Word Practice — red

Read the sentence and color the picture.

I saw a red flower.

Cut and paste to spell the sight word.

red

e d r

Red Word Practice — make

Red Word Practice — little

Read the sentence and color the picture.

The kitten is little.

Cut and paste to spell the sight word.

little

t e t i l l

Red Word Practice — help

Read the sentence and color the picture.

The girl came to help me.

Cut and paste to spell the sight word.

help

e h l p

Red Word Practice down

Read the sentence and color the picture.

Many trees fell down.

Cut and paste to spell the sight word.

down

w d n o

Red Word Practice play

Read the sentence and color the picture.

I like to play with monkeys.

Cut and paste to spell the sight word.

play

a y l p

Red Word Practice - yellow

Read the sentence and color the picture.

I saw a yellow butterfly.

Cut and paste to spell the sight word.

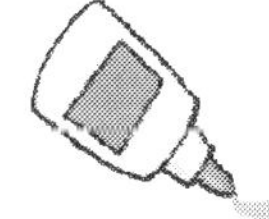

yellow

l e w o y l

Made in the USA
Columbia, SC
26 May 2023

17307917R00070